Witold Lutoslawski

Variations on a Theme by Paganini

for Two Pianos

Chester Music

MW01012780

Wariacje na temat Paganiniego

WITOLD LUTOSŁAWSKI

(1941)

CH55044

4

6

Witold Lutoslawski

Variations on a Theme by Paganini

for Two Pianos

Chester Music

Wariacje na temat Paganiniego

WITOLD LUTOSLAWSKI
(1941)

Allegro capriccioso (♩=ca 144)

CH55044

5

Più mosso (♩= ca 144)

Selected
CONTEMPORARY PIANO MUSIC

PIANO SOLO

Lennox Berkeley
Five Short Pieces
Four Piano Studies
Six Preludes
Sonata

Edvard Hagerup Bull
Variantes *Multi-Métriques*

Niels Viggo Bentzon
Short Pieces Op. 436

Brian Chapple
Trees Revisited

Brian Elias
Five Pieces for the Right Hand

Manuel de Falla
Allegro de Concierto

Fritz Chr. Gerhard
Sieben Aphorismen

Magne Grov
Four Norwegian Folktunes

Peter Maxwell Davies
Sub Tuam Protectionem
Ut Re Mi
Sonata

Arne Nordheim
Listen

Per Nørgård
Achilles and the Tortoise
Turn

Steen Pade
Florilegium

Anthony Payne
Paean
Miniature Variation

Poul Rouders
Dante Sonata (Piano Sonata No. 1)

Robert Saxton
Ritornelli and Intermezzi
Sonata

Philip Wilby
Roses for the Queen of Heaven

PIANO DUET

Lennox Berkeley
Palm Court Waltz
Sonatina

Thea Musgrave
Excursions

TWO PIANOS

Lennox Berkeley
Bagatelle
Polka, Nocturne and Capriccio

Brian Elias
L'Eylah

Witold Lutoslawski
Paganini Variations

Robert Saxton
Sonatas

FOUR PIANOS

Carol Barratt
Four Good-Humoured Variations
on *Ilkley Moor*

Brian Chapple
Scherzos

PIANO(S) AND ORCHESTRA*

Lennox Berkeley
Concerto in B flat
Concerto for two pianos

Brian Chapple
Piano Concerto

Eugene Goossens
Phantasy Concerto

André Previn
Piano Concerto

John Tavener
Palintropos

Solo parts with orchestral reductions available

CHESTER MUSIC

Ancora più mosso (♩ = ca 88)

Selected
CONTEMPORARY PIANO MUSIC

PIANO SOLO

Lennox Berkeley
Five Short Pieces
Four Piano Studies
Six Preludes
Sonata

Edvard Hagerup Bull
Variantes *Multi-Metriques*

Niels Viggo Bentzon
Short Pieces Op. 436

Brian Chapple
Trees Revisited

Brian Elias
Five Pieces for the Right Hand

Manuel de Falla
Allegro de Concierto

Fritz Chr. Gerhard
Sieben Aphorismen

Magne Grov
Four Norwegian Folktunes

Peter Maxwell Davies
Sub Tuam Protectionem
Ut Re Mi
Sonata

Arne Nordheim
Listen

Per Nørgård
Achilles and the Tortoise
Turn

Steen Pade
Florilegium

Anthony Payne
Paean
Miniature Variation

Poul Rouders
Dante Sonata (Piano Sonata No. 1)

Robert Saxton
Ritornelli and Intermezzi
Sonata

Philip Wilby
Roses for the Queen of Heaven

PIANO DUET

Lennox Berkeley
Palm Court Waltz
Sonatina

Thea Musgrave
Excursions

TWO PIANOS

Lennox Berkeley
Bagatelle
Polka, Nocturne and Capriccio

Brian Elias
L'Eylah

Witold Lutoslawski
Paganini Variations

Robert Saxton
Sonatas

FOUR PIANOS

Carol Barratt
Four Good-Humoured Variations
on *Ilkley Moor*

Brian Chapple
Scherzos

PIANO(S) AND ORCHESTRA*

Lennox Berkeley
Concerto in B flat
Concerto for two pianos

Brian Chapple
Piano Concerto

Eugene Goossens
Phantasy Concerto

André Previn
Piano Concerto

John Tavener
Palintropos

Solo parts with orchestral reductions available

CHESTER MUSIC